Color My Mandalas 2

LOUISE ATHERTON

2017 Louise Atherton
louiseathertoncoloring.wordpress.com

All rights reserved.
ISBN: 1545232210
ISBN-13: 978-1545232217

LOUISE ATHERTON

Narrow

LOUISE ATHERTON

Devour

COLOR MY MANDALAS 2

LOUISE ATHERTON

Embrace

LOUISE ATHERTON

Touch

LOUISE ATHERTON

Kiss

Starting

COLOR MY MANDALAS 2

Falling

LOUISE ATHERTON

Knowing

Tremble

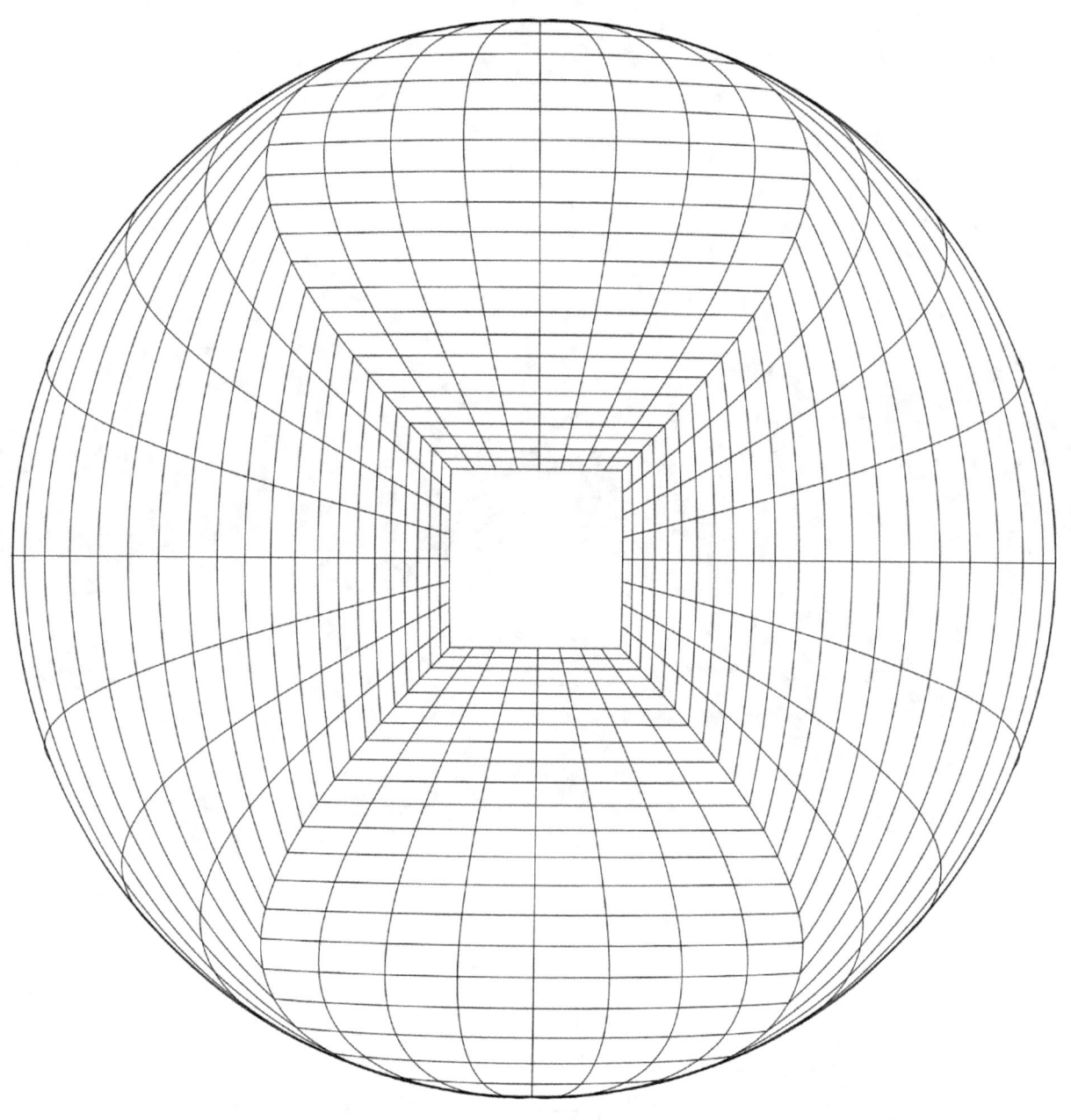

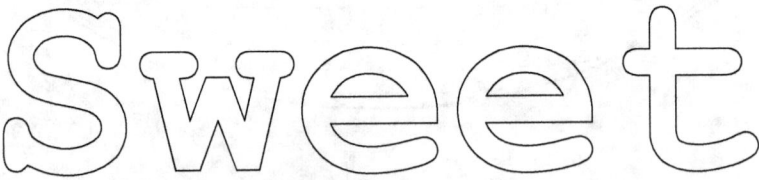

LOUISE ATHERTON

Compassionate

Tranquility

LOUISE ATHERTON

Stability

LOUISE ATHERTON

Placid

Serenity

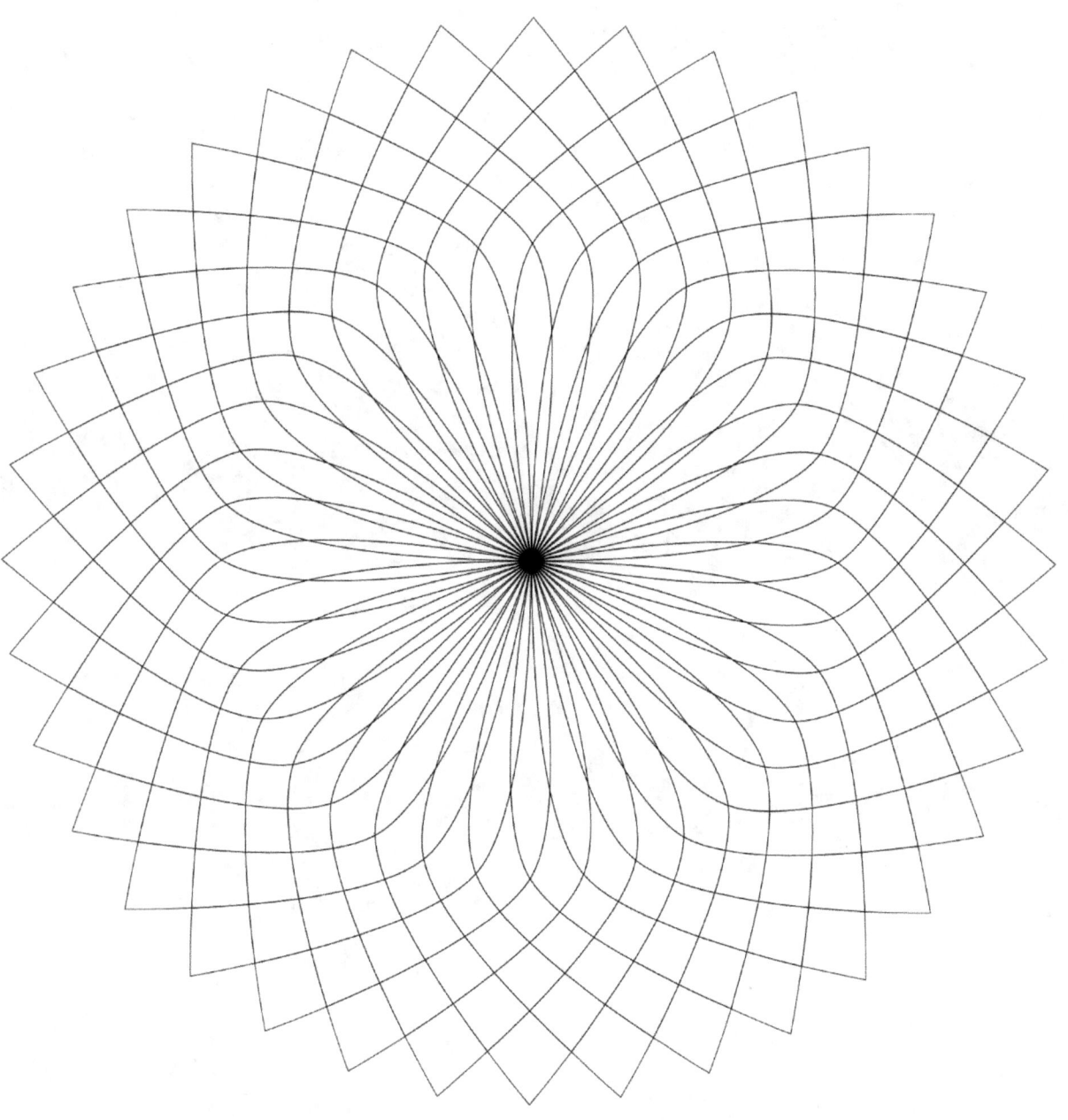

LOUISE ATHERTON

Sympathy

Empathy

LOUISE ATHERTON

Feat

LOUISE ATHERTON

Revelation

LOUISE ATHERTON

Reveal

Smooth

Pleasing

LOUISE ATHERTON

Sweetness

Pleasure

LOUISE ATHERTON

Homesick

LOUISE ATHERTON

Slumber

… LOUISE ATHERTON

Warmth

Nostalgia

LOUISE ATHERTON

Grasp

LOUISE ATHERTON

Wishing

www.ingramcontent.com/pod-product-compliance
Lightning Source LLC
Chambersburg PA
CBHW081122180526
45170CB00008B/2966